Cold
Coffee

Yakari GABRIEL

Cold
Coffee

VOL. 1

POEMS AND THOUGHTS

For my mother, my cousins, my teacher Stephanie and all the other women who taught me I could. To the protagonists of these poems, who even when dead still gave me poetry. Everything of mine is yours.

Contents

Foreword

For all those times someone asked me "Please help me understand Yakari" and I never found the right words, or was too embarrassed to admit doubt, and let the battered and bruised parts show. For the soft side too, the tangible sadness, the overwhelming sensitivity and I could go on. If they were to ask me again, I would hand them this book and say: "Here read this, it's an open letter to the girl you once were."

I met Yakari Gabriel in Aruba about four years ago in a small Cuban Restaurant where we held a monthly poetry night for the Poets' Society, and she shook everyone to their core when she spoke. Even though as far as I recall, it was the first time I had ever laid eyes on her it felt like I have known her much longer as if my heart recognized her voice from some past story I have lived.

She's pure power, presence, precision, and feelings. Not

just because she knows exactly how to pull each heartstring with her clever play on words and her majestic metaphors, but because she means it all, and it resonates true in each sentence.

Yakari's raw and complex storytelling grabs you by the face and makes you face the mirror; it keeps you there longer because, under her spell, you find the courage you never had before to look. She plays her four languages like secret trump cards, emerging from under her sleeve, to season and sprinkle sazon over poetry. She embodies the new Caribbean voice, with her immigrant background; she proudly wears on her sleeve.

Yakari is the hero in her own story, the curly-haired wonder who will hand you back your internal personal glory with each carefully crafted rhyme. Like a gatekeeper to your emotions, she chases you with her narrative, taps on the shoulder, just as you are ready to walk away and says: "Hey is this yours?" And you take it from Yakari and thank her because you couldn't have said it better, and consequently, you will never really forget her again.

Maria Silva

Poems and Thoughts

A Thought

Some women
Need to disappear
In order to heal
So let them go.

After You

After you, I tried
I can promise you I did
In every set of brown eyes
That I found under every rock
Behind every shadow.

After you, I stumbled everywhere
I kissed every set of lips
That were forbidden during
you And even before you
I slept with one, with two
Trying to feel beautiful one more time.

But no body, ever felt like yours
And nothing as intimate as having
You on the corner of my bed
Watching me from the corner of your eyes.

I lied to myself a million times
But after you, I didn't love again.

Belief System

At the end of the day
My intuition
Is my God
It is my faith
When confusion
Comes and shakes me
It remains strong
Settled
In the middle
Of the chest
The only one
I am sure I can trust.

Body

I never thought
Your body
Would be
The cure for
My wanderlust.

Brilliance

The teacher will know you are brilliant before anyone

else She won't say it to your face but you will

Hear her comment on it from across the hallway

The boy you think loves you might stay

But only if he decides he can deal with all your glory

Your mother will slap you across the face too many

Times throughout your lifetime

She will hate; the power inside your

voice But you will cope, you'll be okay

Life will teach you early on That

carrying too many strengths

Comes with a high price to pray.

"You" a miracle in your own right. May all the lights of my love keep you safe, when the dark of the world creeps in.

Bruised

You not wanting me

Might have bruised my ego

But it paved the way for self-love.

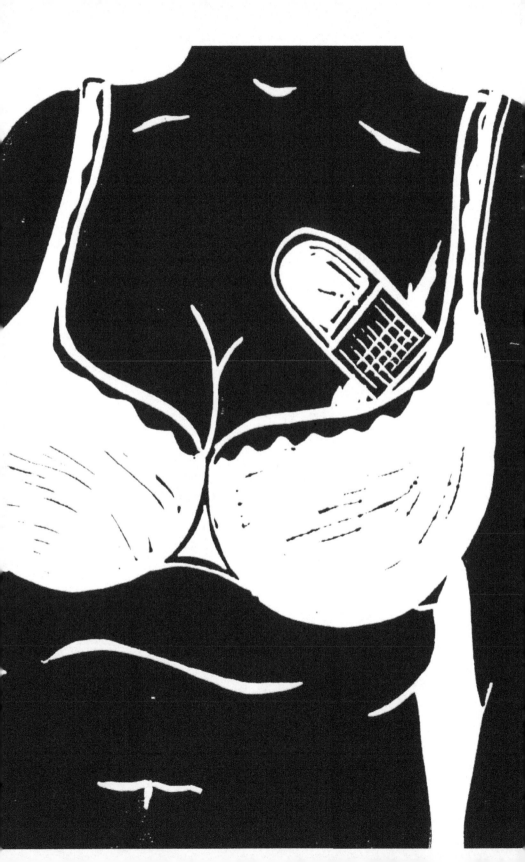

Change

Love, always

Finds me in a way

And leaves me in another.

Choice

I did crumble;
I broke beneath
The weight of all
Those lovers
You chose over me.

Comfortable

People tell you
To embrace the sad
To let it run its course
They rarely warn you
About the possibility
Of it getting comfortable with you
Of it warming you up in bed at night
So much, you sit at home
Waiting for it to come back
So much, you go looking for it
When it takes too long to arrive.

Commitment

I love Love

But Love doesn't love

Women that won't commit

And saying 'no' is all I know

How to do.

Courage

I was reading Anna Nicole Smith's biography
How the media says she overdosed, but the father
of Her daughter said she died of a broken heart
How the high of having a daughter and the low
of Days after burying her son was what pushed
her To the arms of death.

My whole life I've been questioning
Why my mother was so cruel to me
Why her love just stung so bad
But my mother's brother drowned
And they never saw the body
She raised his kids.

Then her sister died after losing her
Seven-year-old son
Next to her on a hospital bed
She told me about how she had
Her hand in her hand, when her nails

Started to turn blue
She had to grief her nephew
Grief her sister
And take in the other kids.

My grandmother had breast cancer
My mother swears my grandfather caused
it Because he used to beat her so much
My grandmother died three months after I was
Born. She was just waiting on me
So she didn't leave my mother alone
Mama told me that before dying
She put her hand on her shoulder
Told her "valor Rubia, valor"
Translates to "courage Rubia, courage"
Maybe courage is more important than love
Maybe that's why the women in my family
Are more courageous than they are loving.

Love can't save a family, but courage does.

Mama, para agradecerte lo que haz hecho por mi en esta vida, necesitaría cien vidas más,

Mother, I would need a hundred more lives, to thank you for what you have done for me in this lifetime.

Photograph by Anuar Habibe

Eryn

She a mouthful of holy water.

-six-word story

For The Lonely

I pray one day you wake up
And your phone isn't the first
Thing you reach for in bed.

There are a lot of people out there who made their dreams come true. I knew I had to be one of them. Sharing a picture of me with Alysia Harris is honoring the woman who made me pick up the microphone and give the poems a voice. It was all a dream…

For the Most Part

Mostly;
I think that I am
Going to die alone
No one will cry –
They will bury me
With my hair tied
Because alive, my curls
Always hid my face
Maybe after death
They'll be no more shame
Behind my eyes.

Mostly, I think that my womb will remain intact
That it will dry up, it would not stretch for any life
That I will live up until I am 45
With my friends around me reminding me
That I never gave love a yes.

They'll be no need for an autopsy
They'll be no need to know
Whose skin was last
Beneath my nails
Wherever you put me -
I was never known for being
One that touched many bodies
Though I know more than you think.

I think, that the end will be tragically beautiful
That life after this one is a dream so good
People never wake up again
For the most part, I am not afraid of anything
Except for staying alive too long
Even after, all my dreams have died.

Forgiveness

When I was smaller
My mother's palms
Always knew how to find my face
There was always an object
Close enough to her, always looked
Like it could meet my back
Or my knees or my head.

Growing up
Someone was always screaming
Always saying; you're gonna kill her
Always someone trying to stop a fight
When my words were inappropriate
Her fist would block my mouth
Always saying things like;
"o te haces gente, o te mueres"
"Yo no voy a criar un parasito".

This is the reason

I am so good with words nowadays

This is the reason

People are impressed when they meet me

This is the reason

I always know what to say

This is why I am so tough yet so human.

I'm tougher than most

Because the mediocrity

Was literally beaten out of me

God knows what I would have been

You don't stand where I am

Therefor you can't see

The beating never beat me

The beating made me.

Authors note: "o te haces gente, o te mueres" is a Dominican expression for turning out decent. And "Yo no voy a criar un parásito" means I am not going to raise a parasite

Free for All

The problem was
That for you
My heart became
An open door
For me it meant
You could come in
But for you it meant
You could leave
When you pleased.

Hands

Just fingers
Just hands
That sometimes
Cry alone
Because they
Can't touch you.

Home

The heart does not
Forget the truth
It knows where
It comes from.

Hypocrite

I used to tell her
"run away from what hurts you"
Until I too, found something
That hurt me but still made me stay.

Identical

It's all a facade
There is no difference
Between a hot woman
And a cold one
Fire burns baby
But have you ever
Had ice rest for
Too long on your skin?
Fire burns baby
But so does ice.

here is a woman... I am on my way to becoming,

she is the woman of my dreams.

Intimacy

Just know that

I am indeed

A masochist

That I know

Pain so well

I can tell

You exactly

What she smells like

What she taste like

Hell, I can even tell

You where

To touch her

If you want

To make her come.

In Pieces

Someone had just jumped in front of the train; I was in when you called, I felt everything beneath my feet. My heart was trying to catch its breath, 'may angels lead you in' I whisper to myself. The train stops for two whole hours. A woman cries hysterically, two girls tell her it's okay.

My eyes get watery as I think of my childhood. I think of your mental absence, and your violent presence. I think of my father, of the last time I saw him. I question when was the last time someone showed consideration and accountability for the way they hurt me.

Someone wants to love me. I dodge her messages. I tell myself; other women would not cure my mommy issues. I run after someone I want to love, she dodges me. It's forbidden ground. I'm a walking contradiction.

I send digital kisses to a married man. We talk about haram thoughts. He is Muslim; I think he's a woman inside. I only believe in universal vibration. I try to forgive myself for lusting. He said I am kind. He said I am funny. I feel appreciated for once.

My hair validates my beauty too often, to the point I don't feel like anything when I tie it up. One of these days, I might shave it off.

Justifying My Vices

By now I am starting to think

That having a boiling desire for

Things that are already taken Is

an inherited trait.

I was conceived by

Cheating anyways

To say I'm against it

Would be self-hate.

Leaving

You left, but I kept myself.

-six word story

Like Trees

We are the women
Who grew up seeing
All the other women cry
And were determined
To not tell the same story
This is why we don't call
This is why we don't text back
We build our own houses
We buy our own drinks
We choose heartbreak
Over loneliness
Over and over again
Like trees, we die standing.

Love isn't Always the Answer

She loves me though

And I love her too

I love her a lot

But love isn't always the answer

Is not always the cure

Can't always be the band aid

For wounds that need stitches.

Expert from: "to the white lady with the big heart"

No One Else

But how was I
Going to learn
To love anyone else?
You claimed this body
Like a land
Like you
Were a colonizer
Of some sort
I barely remember
The language
I spoke before you
What I did
On Saturday mornings
What I celebrated
And why
You are the only
Thing I know
The only thing
I seem to understand
Perfectly.

Notes of Summer

Even if it fades eventually

Even if we end up in a tragedy

I'll keep alive the memory

For a moment, we were so

So beautiful, I did not...

Even want to put

My hands on it.

Sacred Place

My body has been
Around darling
But your mind
Is the most
Beautiful place
I have ever visited.

Self Defense is Not Ingratitude

'Don't bite the hands that feeds you'

That's true

But, when the hand that feeds you

Starts abusing you

When it starts to spit

In your face

Don't only bite

Bite hard-

Run

Rise

And get your own food.

Shame

Still,
I want to know
What it is like
To write about
This pain without
Feeling shame
Simply because
It is here.

Shine

Have you seen
The size of the sky?
Can you measure where
It starts or where it ends?
Don't let anyone tell you
There is no room for you
To be a star.

Stay

I would tell you
To skip the crazy
To meet me
At the corner of 30
When I've passed
The madness
But love don't
Work like that
If you skip the bad
You'll miss the essence
So stay, please stay
I'm on the edge of becoming
I want you to see it front row.

The Alchemist

You do not know

Where I've made

It out of-

You do not know

What I'm still

Going through

But, you still

Look at me

Like I am the

Epitome

Of strength

Maybe poets

Are magicians

In disguise

After all.

The Fear

I fear this feeling
As hard as
I love you
Fear that you'll
Find out, just how
Much of an animal
I can be
When I go
From poet to woman
From friend to lover
When these short writes
Turn into scriptures-
When my claws
Come out
And I scar you
Just to mark territory
Just to let them know
You're mine.

The Moon

Perhaps, you look

In the mirror

And only notice

The holes

The cracks

The broken door

Someone left behind

When they forced

Their way out

But I look at you

And see the light

That came in

Through all those

Open spaces

My love

From where

I am standing

You look

Like the moon.

To my Daughter

On your birthdays
I will only give you
Stories and dolls
Of women who
Look like you.

My Goddaughter Felishah, one day I will tell you the story of how we met, and how I stayed alive, to not miss out seeing you. You're forever my hero.

Too Early

Love is
Way stronger
Than shame
But I didn't
Know that
At the time
We loved.

Too Much

This world wants
To attach our worth
To things that can change
At any given moment
Like our bodies
Our hair
Our faces
Under this type of
Pressure, what else
Could we have become
But insecure, but needy
Or vulnerable.

-To those who claimed that; women want too much

Want

All I ever wanted was a love that was kind.

With Time

Eventually
You're going to find yourself
A woman that is voiceless
She'll be so vacant
Probably drive you to madness
Complaining About
Vain things; like nails
When you go to the store, you'll pay
She'll wait for you to do everything
Kiss you in front of everyone else
And give thanks in obnoxious ways
You'll debate with her often
And she will always let you win
She'll be everything
You thought women should be
But when you start to view her dreams
And realize she has none outside of you
…You'll miss me.

14.09.2017 I didn't celebrate my 24th. It was gloomy,

gray and cold outside. I was in my room busy beating myself up over failing school subjects. I thought there was nothing to celebrate. My friend brought me an apple pie. She took this picture. I shared it on social media with a cocky caption. Because; you know, some people are good at being broken and even better at hiding it.

Acknowledgments

My whole life I've been running around in circles. When I wasn't running, I was writing. These writings are the only thing in this world that belongs to me.

For the woman, the immigrant, the daughter, the hedonist. This is how they came together. I wasn't going to publish; I didn't want strangers holding me in their lap. I did not want to trust them with all of this intimacy. Yet, here I am, swallowing my pride like I often do.

And, finally, my warmest gratitude to Josianne Coutino, Zahira Zaandam, Maria Silva, Michelle Hooyboer and the loyal fans for their patience, love and never ending support—this poetic volume is for you to keep.

Made in the USA
Coppell, TX
31 January 2021